THE CHEESE PLATTER

PHOTOGRAPHY AND DESIGN
By KOREN TRYGG
TEXT BY LUCY POSHEK

ANTIOCH GOURMET
GIFT BOOKS

Published by Antioch Publishing Company
Yellow Springs, Ohio 45387

ISBN 0-89954-828-8

THE CHEESE PLATTER

Printed and bound in the U.S.A.

CONTENTS

A HISTORY OF CHEESE

It is said that cheese was first discovered over six thousand years ago when a nomad poured his milk into an animal pouch. After crossing the desert, he was surprised to find his milk had turned into a thick white mass surrounded by watery fluid—curds and whey. The heat, the sloshing movement, and the natural enzymes present in the pouch had created the first cheese.

Milk made its real leap toward immortality when a shepherd stored his lunch of fresh cheese in a cool cave and forgot to retrieve it. He returned weeks later to find that the cheese had hardened and was covered with a blue vein-like mold. Thus, the process of curing, or aging, cheeses began.

Cheese became a valued staple among the ancient civilizations. Most Roman households kept a *caseale*, or cheese kitchen, as well as curing rooms. By the first century A.D., agricultural writers were already recording detailed accounts of cheesemaking.

During the Dark Ages, European monasteries became the centers of cheesemaking. The monks invented and produced a great assortment of cheeses, such as Port du Salut and Roquefort. By the fifteenth century, the cheesemaking process had developed into a finely tuned art.

But cheesemaking remained on a small scale—mostly in the realm of the home and farms—until more advanced equipment was designed over the nineteenth century. In 1851, the world's first cheese factory was established in New York. By 1865, over five hundred cheese factories had been built in the state of New York alone. Four years later, two-thirds of all the cheese made in the United States came from factories.

The twentieth century saw the invention of still more cheeses such as Double and Triple Crèmes and Cream cheese. Pasteurized cheese and process cheese (a pasteurized blend of natural cheese, fillers, and emulsifiers) were both discovered by James L. Kraft in 1916. Although considered a non-cheese by most connoisseurs, the mild taste and good keeping quality of process cheese made it enormously popular.

Fine gourmet shops now enable us to sample an intriguing variety of cheeses from all over the world. But there remain hundreds of small farm cheeses that never reach the market. Cheese-tasting is a veritable treasure chest of discovery and new surprises.

Early Roman children were often rewarded by their parents with gifts of little cheeses.

CHEESEMAKING

The key to natural cheesemaking is *curdling*—separating the curd (the solid part of milk) from the whey (the liquid). To initiate curdling, the milk must be heated, churned, and soured—sometimes with a starter. The soured milk is then activated by an enzyme called rennet. Rennet causes soured milk to separate into curds and whey.

Once the curd reaches a custard-like firmness, it is cut into small pieces to separate the whey. For soft, moist cheeses, the curd is hardly cut at all; for hard cheeses, it is cut into little pieces to expel more of the whey.

The curd is then drained of its whey. At home, this is done by wrapping the curd in cheesecloth and hanging it up; in factories, draining is usually done in a big vat. After adding salt and sometimes other flavorings, the curd is pressed into a mold to further drain out any moisture.

Almost all cheeses begin with this same preparation. At this point they have little or no flavor. That is why most fresh, unaged cheeses, such as Cottage cheese, taste very mild. Each cheese gets its distinct character from the way it is aged, cured, or ripened.

The length of time a cheese ages greatly affects the final product. Mild or young cheeses—the softest—are aged two to three months. Mellow cheeses age up to six months. Sharp or aged cheeses are cured for more than six months and have the hardest texture. This sharpness is caused by bacteria that grows during the aging process. Sometimes additional cultures—mold, bacteria, or yeast—are added to the interior or exterior during the curing stage, as is the case with blue-veined cheeses and soft-ripening cheeses such as Brie and Camembert. And sometimes the rinds are washed with brine.

Endless variations of this process have developed over time. Many small factors—the kind of milk (cow, goat, or sheep; whole or skim; raw or pasteurized), temperature of the milk, flavorings and molds added, time spent pressing and curing—all result in a distinctive type of cheese. Even the season and time of day when an animal is milked can affect the flavor.

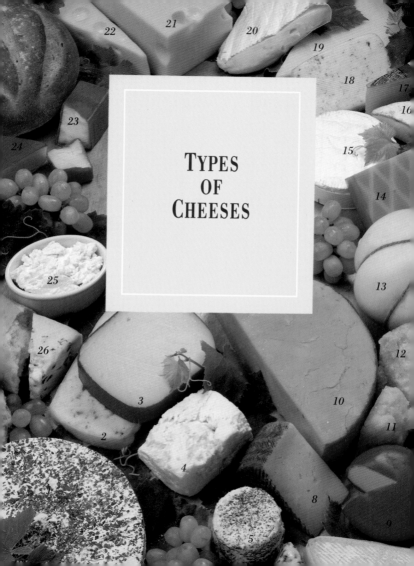

TYPES
OF
CHEESES

TYPES OF CHEESES

1. Brie with herbs
2. New Holland garden vegetable
3. Edam
4. Feta
5. Chèvre with herbs
6. Roquefort
7. French Brie
8. Manchengo (Sheep)
9. Baby Gouda
10. English Cheddar
11. Romano
12. Parmesan
13. Mozzarella
14. Smoked Cheddar
15. Baby Brie
16. French Double Crème
17. Old Amsterdam
18. Havarti with dill
19. Fontina
20. Camembert
21. Swiss
22. Jarlsberg
23. Vermont Cheddar
24. Holland Gouda
25. Farmer's
26. Bleu

*"How can you be expected to govern
a country that has two hundred and
forty-six kinds of cheese?"*

CHARLES DE GAULLE

13

FRESH CHEESES

Fresh cheeses, also called Country cheeses, involve little, if any, aging. They are usually soft, white, moist, and perishable, with a very mild flavor.

Cottage—Sometimes known as Popcorn cheese, Cottage cheese is made from pasteurized skim milk. Sold with either large or small curds. Lower in fat and calories than any other cheese.

Cream—Made with cream or a mix of cream and milk. Available plain, flavored, and whipped. Cream cheese is used in many ways with other foods and as a common spread in the U.S. To serve as an appetizer, cut a one-inch slice and garnish the top with cayenne pepper, dill leaves, or a layer of inexpensive caviar.

Mozzarella—Fresh, unaged Mozzarella, sometimes called *Bufala*, is pure white and usually sold while still soaking in its liquid. Extremely tender and juicy, its delicate flavor is nothing less than sublime when served with sliced tomatoes and basil. Originally made in southern Italy from water buffalo's milk; now usually made from cow's milk.

Ricotta—Some purists classify Ricotta as a non-cheese since it is made from whey instead of milk. Nonetheless, Ricotta has a consistency similar to Cottage cheese; in fact, they are interchangeable in cooking. Also delicious when served with fruit as a dessert.

Feta—Originally made in the Eastern Mediterranean from raw sheep's milk. Now Feta comes from all types of milk. Cured for a few days up to four weeks. Sometimes sold soaked in brine, which keeps it from drying out. Tangy, salty flavor. Excellent crumbled in salads; with figs, crusty breads, tomatoes, and light red wines.

Farmer's—In the U.S. this is a pressed, hard cheese; in France, it is more like Cottage cheese. Slightly sour flavor. Most Farmer's cheeses are better for cooking than on the table. Easy to make at home.

Chèvres—Any French goat cheeses. White, soft body. Slight buttermilk flavor. Chèvres made exclusively from goat's milk are marked *pur chèvre*.

Neufchâtel—In the U.S., only ripened Neufchâtel—both flavored and plain—is usually sold. In France, fresh Neufchâtel is often served with strawberries or green grapes and a semisweet wine. Soft, creamy consistency with less fat than Cream cheese.

Mascarpone—Increasingly popular Italian cheese made from fresh cream. Looks like clotted cream—thick and rich, with a sweet, delicate flavor. Available only in specialty stores. Usually served as a dessert in Italy—with fruit, sugar, and liqueur—and as the main ingredient in *tiramisu*.

SOFT-RIPENING
BLOOMY RIND CHEESES

Soft-ripening, or surface-
ripened, cheeses are cured by applying mold, bacteria or
yeast to the surface of the cheese. Soft-ripening cheeses

such as Brie and Camembert are sprayed or rubbed with mold. The enzymes on the surface cause a softening of the curd. Successful curing results in a thin velvety rind—also called a *bloomy* rind.

Aged for only one month, soft-ripening cheeses are extremely delicate and should be eaten within a few days of their peak ripeness. A hint of ammonia in the flavor indicates overripeness; a chalky taste means it's underripe.

The subtle, rich flavor of soft-ripening bloomy rind cheeses should not be overpowered by strong foods. Unsalted water crackers, crusty French bread, grapes, strawberries, and pears are good companions. A dry champagne is considered the best accompaniment, although most red, white, and dessert wines are wonderful, too.

Brie—In 1815, the Congress of Vienna voted Brie as the *Roi de Fromage*, or "King of Cheeses." Originally made in France from cow's whole milk. Creamy, smooth texture with an edible thin white crust. Excellent dessert cheese.

Camembert—Made in France from cow's whole milk for over three hundred years. Luscious, smooth taste with edible rind. Smaller size and slightly different flavor than Brie. A fine Camembert has a hint of mushrooms in its flavor.

French Double or Triple Crèmes—Produced similarly to Camembert but higher in fat content. Boursault and Boursin are two of the best known Triple Crèmes, which have the highest cream content. Boursin is available pepper-coated, or with garlic and herbs.

17

SOFT-RIPENING
WASHED RIND CHEESES

These cheeses are made in much the same manner as soft-ripening bloomy rind cheeses except that their surface is ripened by bacteria and yeast instead of mold. They are washed regularly with salty water (brine), dried and turned during their six- to eight-week curing time. This process results in a *washed rind*.

Most of the cheeses originally produced in monasteries, such as Port du Salut, are still made in this way. Monterey Jack, a difficult cheese to classify, would best fit in this category also.

These types of cheeses have firmer bodies than soft-ripening bloomy rind cheeses, and their flavor ranges from mild to very pungent. The milder varieties are good on a cheese board with neutral fruits such as pears and green grapes, water crackers or melba toast. The stronger-tasting washed rind cheeses go well with many foods. Try fruity white wines with the current-aged cheeses; light reds with the stronger varieties.

Port du Salut—First made by Trappist monks around 1865 at the Abbey at Port du Salut in France. By now the making of Port du Salut has spread to other monasteries in Europe and the U.S., but the Trappists have kept the exact process a secret. Any of these cheeses made outside Port du Salut are called St. Paulin. Semihard texture and mild, buttery flavor.

Muenster—First made in France, then Germany, and now much imitated in the U.S., where it is very popular. American Muenster is milder and creamier than German Muenster.

Brick—Made in Wisconsin. Strong when aged. May need an acquired taste.

Limburger—Original Belgian cheese now made in Germany. Strongest-smelling and -tasting of all cheeses. Sometimes called the "stinking cheese." Needs an acquired taste. Best with ale and assertive red wines.

BLUE-VEINED CHEESES

When Emperor Charlemagne was first presented with Roquefort cheese at a French monastery, he began scraping away the blue veins until the monks suggested that the veins were the most prized part. So the emperor tried it, veins and all, and loved Roquefort so much that he ordered a yearly supply from the monastery.

Wide-spread veining in blue-veined cheeses is still considered a sign of good flavor. The veins are created by the injection of a mold that spreads through the cheese. The blue-green streaks give each cheese its spicy flavor.

Blue-veined cheeses are best served with unsalted crackers, French bread, celery, green grapes, figs, and assertive red wines. They are also delicious when crumbled into salads and soups.

Roquefort—Real Roquefort, made from whole sheep's milk and cured in the caves of Roquefort village, is marked with a Red Sheep seal. The blue mold powder that is placed between the layers of Roquefort curd is derived from ground-up loaves of aged bread that have been injected with pure mold culture. The cheeses are punctured with holes to promote mold growth and then stored in underground caves for two to five months. The result is a sharp, spicy, fairly salty flavor.

Bleu or Blue—Bleu is the name for a group of Roquefort-type cheeses made in France from milk other than sheep's milk. If produced in the U.S., it is called Blue cheese and is made from cow's or goat's milk. Danish Blue cheese, also called Danablu, is a popular, milder variety.

Gorgonzola—Said to have been made in the Po Valley of Italy for over a thousand years. Strongest-tasting of the blue-veined cheeses. Spicy, pungent flavor. Fine dessert cheese.

Stilton—One of the finest of English cheeses. Dates back to the seventeenth century. Milder than Roquefort or Gorgonzola. Rich, smooth, and spicy. Dark, wrinkled rind and slightly flaky texture. Made from whole cow's milk. Should be ripened four to six months. Try with aged port.

The ability to make cheese was referred to as "a gift of everlasting value" in early Greek mythology.

DUTCH CHEESES

Dutch-type cheeses are made from cow's milk into a semisoft curd that is often flavored with herbs and spices such as caraway and cumin. Special molds give Dutch cheeses their famous round and spherical shapes. They are usually aged for two to six months and have a rather porous texture.

Although Edam and Gouda are the most notable cheeses in this category, not all Dutch-type cheeses are made in the Netherlands. Other Dutch-type varieties, such as Danish Havarti and Tilsit, are made elsewhere in Europe.

On the cheese board, Dutch cheeses go well with Concord grapes, pears, cherries, beer, and mild red wines. In sandwiches, they are suited to most any type of bread. Young Dutch cheeses are usually used for cooking, in soufflés and omelettes.

Gouda—Smooth texture and mild yet distinct taste. Cured two to six months with a wax coating. Baby Gouda is a smaller version of the same cheese, usually rolled into a wheel or ball. Smoked gouda is very flavorful.

Edam—The Dutch town of Alkmaar, where Edam is sold by the last medieval guild in existence, is a major summer tourist attraction. Edam is also made in the U.S. now. Real Dutch Edam should have a six-sided mark on

the outside of the rind that says "Holland." Firm, elastic body. Mild, clean flavor. Contains less fat than Gouda.

Danish Havarti and Tilsit—Danish Havarti was formerly called Danish Tilsit. They are both often confused with German Tilsit, which is similar but has a stronger, more controversial flavor. Danish Havarti is porous, semihard, and sometimes spiced with caraway.

In the medieval cheese markets of Europe, only the wealthy could afford the largest wheels of cheese. Those people with enough money to buy the biggest wheels were called "big wheels" or "big cheeses."

MOZZARELLA & PROVOLONE

Made from cow's milk, these cheeses are known in Italy as *pasta filata*, or plastic curd. After the curd is separated from the whey, the curd is immersed in hot whey and then hot water. The heat makes the curd tough and elastic. It is worked and stretched into a plastic, fiber-like condition, then chilled in cold water and immersed in brine for several days. Wrapped in cheesecloth, the curd is then tied with twine, suspended to dry, and cured for two to four months.

Mozzarella—Originally made in southern Italy from water buffalo's milk, Mozzarella is now made mostly from cow's milk in the U.S. as well as Italy. (Ricotta comes from the whey of Mozzarella.) Although there is nothing so delicious as fresh, unaged Mozzarella (see Fresh Cheeses), the cured, usually prepackaged variety is one of the most popular cooking cheeses. It is low in fat and melts smoothly, with no greasy residue. Aged Mozzarella has a mild, delicate flavor and rubbery texture.

Provolone—Originally made in southern Italy. Made from skimmed evening milk and whole morning milk, Provolone is smoked before maturing. It is usually sold in a large sausage or pear shape, bound in cord. Provolone cured from six to nine months makes an excellent table and sandwich cheese. Its mildly smoky flavor goes wonderfully with salami, pears, plums, and melon. Like Mozzarella, Provolone tastes best with red wines and dry whites.

SWISS CHEESES

Swiss cheeses have a sweetish, nutty flavor, firm texture, and eyes, or holes. These eyes are caused by bacteria added to the heated milk. While ripening, gases develop from the bacteria and are unable to escape from the interior, resulting in holes. Ripening and eye formation must be uniform throughout the inside of Swiss cheeses. The eyes should "weep" with beads of moisture when cut—a sign of optimum ripeness.

Because of their excellent melting properties, Swiss-type cheeses are recommended for cooking and fondues. As a table cheese, they go well with any breads, pears, and grapes. Most white and light red wines are good accompaniments, as are some champagnes.

Swiss Emmentaler—Originating in Bern, Switzerland in 1280, this is considered the original Swiss cheese. Also called Switzerland Swiss. Made from raw milk. Aged for four to twelve months. Mildly nutty and sweet, with cherry-sized holes. Real Emmentaler has the word "Switzerland" in red on the rind. Perfect for cooking and sandwiches.

Gruyère—Made in Switzerland for centuries. Smaller, softer, and sharper-tasting than Emmentaler, with only a few tiny eyes. One of the best cooking cheeses. Traditional Swiss fondue is made with Emmentaler and Gruyère.

Jarlsberg—Norwegian invention of the late 1950's. Very popular in the U.S. Mild and nutty, with a hint of sweetness.

American Swiss—Mostly made in Wisconsin. Usually aged for only two months. Milder than Emmentaler.

Fontina—Originally from Italy; now made in Denmark and Sweden. Fontina Val d'Aosta is considered the best brand. Has tiny holes, mild taste, and semisoft texture.

Raclette—Spicy yet not overpowering; small eyes. Used in Switzerland for a popular melted cheese dish served with cornichons and boiled potatoes.

The Abbey of Rougemont in Switzerland was built with taxes collected on Gruyère cheese during the Middle Ages.

CHEDDAR CHEESES

Cheddar-type cheeses are made from cow's pasteurized whole milk and usually an orange coloring such as annatto (an extract from a West Indian fruit). In the early days of cheesemaking, carrot juice or crushed marigolds were used to color Cheddar cheeses.

What gives Cheddars their distinctively dense texture is a *cheddaring* process: The curd is sliced into thick slabs, then stacked and restacked to induce matting of the curd.

Cheddars are cured for three months up to a year, and they keep very well. Young Cheddars are mild in flavor; aged Cheddars are sharp.

Aged Cheddars go well with hearty beers or ales and full-bodied red wines. Milder Cheddars are best accompanied with white wines or sherries. Try serving them with fresh farmer's bread, sweet pickles or gherkins, and apples.

Cheddar—This original Cheddar cheese is named for the English village where it was first made in the late sixteenth century. Today, there are many variations of Cheddar, in both Britain and the U.S.

Cheshire—One of the oldest and most popular of the English Cheddar-type cheeses. Cheshire cheeses have an intense, somewhat salty flavor and crumbly texture.

Gloucester—More intense than Cheshire. Has a strong buttermilk taste. Double Gloucester is larger and aged longer than Gloucester.

Leicester—English country cheese with a deep orange color. One of the mildest Cheddars. Used much in cooking.

American Cheddar—Produced in New York, Vermont and Wisconsin, American Cheddars are among the most popular cheeses in the U.S. The best are Herkimer County (New York) and white Vermont Cheddar.

Longhorn—refers loosely to any of the American Cheddar varieties.

Colby—Popular U.S. Cheddar. Made similarly to Cheddar but not matted together. Very mild flavor.

Thomas Jefferson loved Cheddar so much that an immense wheel of it was given to celebrate his inauguration in 1801.
Andrew Jackson placed his inaugural cheese in the hall of the White House, where it was slowly consumed by admirers.

HARD-GRATING CHEESES

Italians call cheeses such as Parmesan and Romano the *grana*, or grain, cheeses. Made in the Po Valley of Italy and now in the U.S., these cheeses have a dry, granular texture and sharp flavor.

Hard-grating cheeses have the longest shelf life and become richer with age. They are usually grated for cooking. However, current-aged real Italian Parmesan and Romano are delicious when thinly sliced and served with fresh Italian bread, prosciutto, melon, and a dry white or full-bodied red wine—all regional specialties of northern Italy.

Parmigiano-Reggiano—This is real Italian Parmesan and considered the best hard-grating cheese in the world. By Italian law, only cheeses made in the region between Parma and Reggio can be called Parmigiano-Reggiano. Known as the "Cheese of Seven Centuries," the formula for Parmigiano-Reggiano hasn't changed in seven hundred years. Unpasteurized evening and morning cow's milk is heated in special copper cauldrons. Must be aged two years before it can be exported. Crumbly texture; spicy, rich taste.

Parmesan—American-made Parmesan, usually from Wisconsin, is an imitation of Italian Parmesan. It is aged for only fourteen months and is generally used only for cooking.

Romano—Also called Pecorino Romano, or Incanestrato, Romano cheese was originally made in Italy from sheep's milk during the first century A.D. Today it is made from cow's and sometimes goat's milk in both Italy and the U.S. Current-aged Romano, cured five to eight months, makes a good table cheese, whereas aged Romano, cured for over a year, is usually grated and used in cooking.

SERVING CHEESE

When presenting cheeses for a dessert, party, or wine-and-cheese-tasting, the usual rule is to select three or four cheeses that vary in flavor, texture, shape, and color. However, you could feature cheeses of one nationality instead—French Brie,

Roquefort, and Chèvre, for example. Or, you could serve cheeses of one type, such as a variety of Cheddars. This enables your guests the chance to taste, side by side, the subtle differences within one cheese group.

When preparing a cheese board:

—Arrange the cheeses on a wooden or marble cheese board with garnishes of grape, cabbage, or lettuce leaves; parsley; or fruit. (A sprig of thyme will offset contrasting odors.) Allow ample space between each cheese and a variety of cutting utensils so the flavors won't get mixed together.

—Allow cheeses to come to room temperature before serving so their full flavor is released. For soft cheeses, allow 20 to 30 minutes; for others, allow 1 to 2 hours, depending on the size.

—Leave the cheese rind intact when serving. If it has a wax coating, peel it back like a flower petal.

—Place crackers and breads in a separate basket. Since cheese is already heavily salted, serving salted or strongly-flavored crackers is not usually recommended for a cheese-tasting.

—Wine is the perfect complement to cheese, but if non-alcoholic drinks are requested, offer mild fruit juices, tonic water, club soda with a slice of lime, or plain tea. Do not serve sweet sodas. An espresso without milk can accompany dessert cheeses.

Some Cheshire cheeses are made in cat-shaped molds—the inspiration for the Cheshire cat in Alice in Wonderland.

STORING CHEESE

As a general rule of thumb, soft, fresh cheeses will not last as long as hard, cured cheeses. And, with the exception of the very hard-grating cheeses, pasteurized cheeses will keep better than unpasteurized.

Bloomy rind cheeses such as Brie will deteriorate more quickly than washed rind cheeses such as Muenster, and they should be consumed in three days. Blue-veined cheeses should be eaten within three days to one week. Crèmes are best served the day they are purchased.

Although natural cheeses continue to ripen even when refrigerated, at least refrigeration retards the ripening process somewhat. But once mold develops from overaging, discard the whole cheese.

Never leave a cheese exposed too long or it will dry out. A damp cloth wrapped around the cheese (soft cheeses excluded) will help restore its moisture. Aluminum foil and plastic wrap are also good coverings. Hard-grating cheeses will keep almost indefinitely—years, in fact—if wrapped well.

The ancient rite of "cheese rolling" is held every year on Cooper's Hill, near Gloucester. Decorated cheese wheels bounce downhill, chased by a crowd of children. This ceremony marks the beginning of spring.

Baked Brie with Almonds

1 8-oz. wheel of Brie
⅓ cup (2⅔ fl. oz.)
   sliced almonds

1 tbsp. (¾ Br. tbsp.) butter
3-5 dashes cayenne pepper
salt and pepper

Cut off top rind of Brie. Place in oven-proof serving dish. Let sit at room temperature for 20 minutes. Over low heat, cook almonds in butter, stirring constantly until slightly toasted. Drain; sprinkle with cayenne pepper and salt and pepper to taste. Toss well. Chop nuts, then sprinkle on top of Brie. Bake in a preheated 325°F oven for 8-10 minutes. Serve with crackers.

Fresh Mozzarella Sandwiches

Cut a baguette (long, thin loaf of French bread) into slices of medium thickness. Layer each slice of bread with a thin slice of tomato, fresh Mozzarella cheese, and fresh basil leaf. Arrange on a platter and dribble extra virgin olive oil over the sandwiches.

Americans consume an average of twenty-four pounds of cheese per year. But they still lag behind the French and Greeks, who eat more than thirty-two pounds a year.

Greek Pasta Salad

½ lb. mostaccioli cooked,
drained and cooled
¼ cup (2 fl. oz.) olive oil
1 tbsp. (¾ Br. tbsp.)
lemon juice
¼ tsp. black pepper
¼ tsp. dried oregano
1 small clove garlic, minced

2 diced tomatoes,
seeds removed
2 diced green peppers
10 black olives, pitted
and halved
10 radishes, thinly sliced
2 tbsp. (1½ Br. tbsp.)
chopped parsley
4 oz. Feta cheese, crumbled

*Blend olive oil, lemon juice, pepper, oregano,
and garlic. Chill dressing. Toss all other ingredients
together in a bowl. Toss again with dressing. Serves 4.*

Fettuccine with Prosciutto and Blue Cheese

3 tbsp. (2½ Br. tbsp.) virgin olive oil
2 cloves garlic
6 oz. prosciutto or smoked ham, cut in thin strips
⅓ cup (2⅔ fl. oz.) large, pitted black olives, cut in quarters
12 oz. cooked fettuccine
4 oz. crumbled Blue cheese
4 leaves fresh basil, thinly cut
salt and freshly ground pepper

Heat olive oil in pan. Sauté garlic cloves in oil until golden; remove garlic. Add prosciutto and olives to the garlic oil and toss for 20 seconds. Then toss mixture with hot, cooked fettuccine. Arrange pasta on plates. Sprinkle with crumbled Blue cheese, fresh basil, and salt and pepper to taste. Serves 4 to 6.

Pasta with Cheeses

2 cups (16 fl. oz.) cream or half-and-half (half cream and half whole milk)
½ lb. smoked Gouda cheese, shredded
½ cup (4 fl. oz.) grated Parmesan cheese
⅓ cup (2⅔ fl. oz.) grated Romano cheese
12 oz. cooked fettuccine
4 tsp. (3 Br. tsp.) capers
crushed red chiles, if desired

Heat cream over medium heat. Just before it reaches a boil, blend in shredded smoked Gouda, grated Parmesan, and grated Romano cheeses. When cheeses start to melt, raise heat a little. Bring sauce to boil, stirring constantly. Lower heat. Simmer for 5 minutes, until sauce thickens. Serve immediately over cooked pasta; garnish with capers and, if desired, crushed red chiles. Serves 4 to 6.

The crust of a mature Parmesan is so hard, it is nearly bullet-proof.

Vichyssoise with Stilton

4 tbsp. (3 Br. tbsp.) unsalted butter
white part of 4 leeks, chopped fine
1 onion, chopped fine
4 cups (32 fl. oz.) chicken stock
2 stalks celery, chopped fine
2 potatoes, thinly sliced
1 tsp. (¾ Br. tsp.) thyme
½ tsp. salt
pepper to taste
1 cup (8 fl. oz.) half-and-half (half cream and half
    whole milk)
¼ lb. Stilton or Blue cheese, crumbled

*Melt butter in saucepan; add leeks and onion.
Cook slowly until tender, but not brown. Add stock,
celery, and potatoes. Cook until potatoes are tender.
Purée the soup in small batches in a blender. Add
stock if needed to make 2 cups. Return soup to saucepan; stir in cream, thyme, salt, and pepper. Reheat
over low heat. Pour into bowls; serve topped with
crumbled cheese. If desired, sprinkle with a bit of
parsley, thyme, chives, or dill. Serves 4 to 6.*

*Fortnum & Mason in London keep their
Stilton cheese in the cellars beneath the store,
where they are turned daily and brushed.*

Calzone

Dough

¼ cup (2 fl. oz.) warm water
1 (¼-oz.) package active dry yeast
3 cups (24 fl. oz.) all-purpose flour
1 tsp. (¾ Br. tsp.) salt
¾ cup (6 fl. oz.) cool water
1 tbsp. (¾ Br. tbsp.) honey
2 tbsp. (1½ Br. tbsp.) olive oil
2 tbsp. (1½ Br. tbsp.) cornmeal

Pour warm water into a small bowl; sprinkle yeast over water and stir until dissolved. In a separate bowl, combine flour and salt. In a glass measuring cup, combine cool water, honey and olive oil. Add honey mixture and dissolved yeast to flour in bowl. Stir until dough forms. On a lightly floured surface, knead dough until elastic, adding more flour if necessary. Place dough in a large greased bowl. Turn to coat. Cover bowl with a dry towel and let rise in a warm place for 1 hour or until dough has doubled in bulk.

Punch dough down and let rest for 10 minutes before rolling it out.

Filling

1 cup (8 fl. oz.) marinara sauce (tomato sauce with onions, garlic, and spices)
2 cups (16 fl. oz.) grated Mozzarella cheese
2 cups (16 fl. oz.) sliced raw mushrooms

2 cups (16 fl. oz.) sautéed sliced onions or pepperoni
½ cup (4 fl. oz.) sliced black olives
2 tsp. (1½ Br. tsp.) chopped basil

Preheat oven to 450°F. Grease 2 baking sheets and sprinkle with cornmeal.

In a bowl, combine Mozzarella, mushrooms, pepperoni or sautéed onions, black olives, and basil. Set aside.

Divide dough into 8 equal-sized balls. On a lightly floured surface, roll each piece, one at a time, into a thin, flat circle.

Spread one heaping tablespoon marinara sauce over each circle, 1 inch from the edge. Place ½ cup (4 fl. oz.) filling on half of the circle. Fold uncovered half of dough over filling to make a half circle. Moisten edges of dough with water and pinch them together. Place on pans and bake for 10 to 12 minutes, or until golden brown. Serve hot. Makes 8 calzone.

"Milk gathered in the early morning light is curdled at night, but that of twilight the herdsman puts in wooden vats and brings to the city, or is made into cheese for the winter, having been slightly salted."

VIRGIL, 70-19 B.C.

Cheese and Roasted Pepper Pizza

Dough

Prepare Calzone dough (see page 40) as directed. Divide into 2 balls and roll each into a thin circular or rectangular shape. Place each one on pans that have been greased and sprinkled with cornmeal. Preheat oven to 500°F.

Topping

½ cup (4 fl. oz.) prepared marinara (tomato sauce with onions, garlic, and spices) or pizza sauce

3 red or yellow bell peppers, roasted, peeled, sliced, and marinated in olive oil and vinegar

2 cups (16 fl. oz.) shredded Fontina cheese

2 cups (16 fl. oz.) shredded Mozzarella cheese

3 oz. Chèvre or goat cheese

2 tbsp. (1½ Br. tbsp.) freshly grated Romano cheese

1 tbsp. (¾ Br. tbsp.) capers

Spread marinara sauce over each pizza. Add Fontina and Mozzarella cheeses, then roasted peppers. Garnish with crumbled goat cheese and capers. Bake one pizza at a time on top rack of oven for about 10 minutes. Sprinkle Romano cheese on top.

The first cheese brought to America on the Mayflower was Dutch Edam.

Cheese & Vegetable Flan

9-inch unbaked pie shell
egg white
1¾ cups (14 fl. oz.) Gruyère or Fontina cheese, grated
1 tbsp. (¾ Br. tbsp.) butter or margarine
1 cup (8 fl. oz.) fresh mushrooms, sliced
½ cup (4 fl. oz.) asparagus tips, blanched
3 eggs, slightly beaten
1½ cups (12 fl. oz.) half-and-half (half cream and half
    whole milk)
¼ tsp. nutmeg
½ tsp. salt
⅛ tsp. cayenne pepper
1 Roma tomato, seeded and diced
1 tsp. (¾ Br. tsp.) fresh rosemary, finely chopped (opt.)

*Preheat oven to 450°F. Place unbaked pie shell in a
9-inch quiche or pie pan. Prick sides and bottom of
shell. Brush with egg white. Bake for 5 minutes.
Spread cheese in partially baked pie shell. Sauté
mushrooms in butter over medium heat for 1 minute
until cooked yet firm. Drain well. Layer mushrooms
and asparagus on top of cheese. Mix the eggs with the
half and half, nutmeg, salt, and cayenne pepper.
Pour egg mixture over cheese and vegetables. Place
diced tomatoes on top of filling. Sprinkle with rosemary. Bake 15 minutes at 450°F. Reduce heat to
350°F and cook 10 to 15 minutes longer until filling
sets. Serves 6.*

Manicotti with Spinach

1 10-oz. package frozen chopped spinach, thawed
8 manicotti shells
1 clove garlic, minced
2 tbsp. (1½ Br. tbsp.) olive oil
2 cups (16 fl. oz.) Ricotta or Cottage cheese
¼ cup (2 fl. oz.) grated Parmesan cheese
2 eggs, beaten
2 tbsp. (1½ Br. tbsp.) chopped fresh parsley
salt and pepper to taste
3 cups (24 fl. oz.) marinara sauce (tomato sauce with
   onions, garlic, and spices)

*Boil manicotti shells al dente; drain and cool.
Cook minced garlic in olive oil. Add well-drained spinach (squeezing out excess moisture). Cook 2 minutes.
Cool. In a bowl combine Ricotta cheese, Parmesan
cheese, beaten eggs, parsley, salt and pepper. Stuff
manicotti shells with spinach mixture. Pour half the
marinara sauce in a baking pan. Arrange stuffed
shells on top; cover with remaining marinara sauce.
Cook in a 350°F oven for 35 to 40 minutes. Serve with
additional Parmesan cheese. Serves 4.*

*Dessert without cheese
is the kiss without the squeeze.*
OLD VICTORIAN SAYING

Blueberry Cream Cheese Loaf

2 cups (16 fl. oz.) flour
¾ cup (6 fl. oz.) sugar
1½ tsp. (1 Br. tsp.) baking
    powder
1½ tsp. (1 Br. tsp.) baking
    soda
dash of salt
3-oz. package Cream cheese

2 tsp. (1½ Br. tsp.) vanilla
2 tsp. (1½ Br. tsp.) lemon
    juice
2 eggs
¼ cup (2 fl. oz.) hot
    melted butter
½ cup (4 fl. oz.) milk
1 cup (8 fl. oz.) fresh or
    frozen blueberries

Preheat oven to 350°F. Combine dry ingredients in bowl. In blender or food processor, blend wet ingredients (in order as listed) until smooth. Pour mixture into bowl with dry ingredients and stir together. Fold in blueberries. Bake in medium-sized greased loaf pan for about 1 hour or until toothpick comes out clean.

The best things in life are Brie.

ANONYMOUS

GRAPHIC DESIGN BY GRETCHEN GOLDIE

PHOTO STYLING BY SUE TALLON

ACKNOWLEDGMENTS

JOE, DORIAN, AND SCHATZI POSHEK